A New True Book

METEORITES

By Paul P. Sipiera

CHILDRENS PRESS®
CHICAGO

Most iron meteorites reveal this unusual crystal pattern when cut, polished, and etched with acid.

PHOTO CREDITS
© Reinhard Brucker–13, 16 (left), 19 (inset), 32 (right)
North Wind Picture Archives–8
Photo–© Michael Newman, 43 (left); © David Young-Wolff, 43 (right)
Photri–© Charles Philip, 27 (bottom right)
Reuters/Bettmann–39
Root Resources–© Doug Sherman, 24; © Mary A. Root, 32 (top and bottom left), 42
© Paul Sipiera–2, 6 (left), 12, 14, 16 (right), 17, 19, 25, 34, 36, 37, 41 (2 photos), 45; Courtesy of NASA, 22 (2 photos), 30
Tom Stack & Associates–© Frank Rossotto, 20
SuperStock International, Inc.–© Otto Done, Cover; © Gerard F. Fritz, 28
Unicorn Stock Photos–© Jim Shippee, 27 (left); © Ronald E. Partis, 27 (top right)
Valan–© Brian Atkinson, 28
Visuals Unlimited–© Science VU, 4; © Michael Shin, 6 (right); © McDonald, 10
COVER: Meteor Crater Arizona, USA

Dedicated to my teachers:
Louis H. Fuchs,
Carleton B. Moore,
Edward J. Olsen

Project Editor: Fran Dyra
Design: Margrit Fiddle

Library of Congress Cataloging-in-Publication Data

Sipiera, Paul P.
    Meteorites / by Paul P. Sipiera.
        p.   cm.–(A New true book)
    Includes index.
    ISBN 0-516-01068-9
    1.   Meteorites–Juvenile literature.   [1.   Meteorites.]
I.   Title.
QB755.2.S57   1994
523.5'.1–dc20   94-10947
                                                          CIP
                                                          AC

TABLE OF CONTENTS

A meteor streaking across the Milky Way in the constellation Sagittarius

WHAT IS A METEORITE?

Look into the night sky. What do you see? Sometimes there is a big, bright moon and many sparkling stars. The brightest "stars" might be planets.

Once in a while, a streak of light may cross the sky. It does not last long, but it can be very bright. Some people call this a "falling star" or a

Meteors appear as bright streaks of light against the background stars (left). Fireballs (right) are the brightest meteors.

"shooting star." But it is not a star at all. It is a meteor—a small piece of rock or metal that has fallen to Earth from space.

A piece of rock or metal is called a meteor only when it passes through Earth's atmosphere. When it is in space, it is called a meteoroid.

A meteoroid travels through the solar system at a very high speed. Once it enters Earth's atmosphere, it heats up from contact with the air. This is called frictional heating. You can feel frictional heating by rubbing your hands together very fast.

Meteors that reach Earth without burning up are called meteorites.

METEOR SHOWERS

Meteor showers can light up the sky like a fireworks display.

Watch the sky for an hour some night when it is dark out. You will see several meteors. During a meteor shower, you may see up to one hundred per hour. Meteor showers occur several times a year. Look at the Perseid meteor shower. It takes place on the night of August 11-12 every year.

Meteor showers are named for the constellation they appear to be coming from. Look at the constellation Perseus during the Perseid meteor shower. You will see the meteors streaking outward from this position in the sky.

Comets are the cause of most meteor showers.

Meteor showers are related to old comets. Comets are made up of ice mixed with dust. They travel in long orbits, or curved paths, around the sun. As a comet passes close to the sun, it begins to melt. After many trips around the sun, it leaves a trail of dust behind it.

Very often, Earth passes through one of these comet-dust trails. This dust produces a swarm of meteoroids. When this happens, we see an unusually large number of meteors for several nights.

Most meteors are small. They are destroyed as they pass through our atmosphere. Only the large ones survive to hit Earth's surface.

A typical stony meteorite with its "thumbprint" surface.

ROCKS FROM SPACE

Meteorites are rocks from space. Those we see in museums look different from most Earth rocks. Some have dents called "thumbprints" on their surface, while others appear smooth.

A meteorite that has fallen recently has a black coating called a fusion crust. This crust formed as the meteorite's surface melted during its fiery plunge through the atmosphere. Now it looks more like a piece of coal.

Newly fallen meteorites have a black crust covering their surface.

13

Stony meteorites turn rusty brown after being on Earth a long time.

Meteorites that have been on Earth for a long time have brown surfaces. They look rusty. Exposure to air and water has changed their color from black to brown.

There are three kinds of meteorites: stony, iron, and stony-iron meteorites. These groups are classified by the amount of metal present in the meteorite.

A stony meteorite is less than 20 percent metal. An iron meteorite is over 80 percent metal. And a stony-iron meteorite is about 50 percent metal and 50 percent stone.

Sometimes stony meteorites look like ordinary rocks (left).
Right: A slice of a meteorite showing the metal in it.

Most meteorites are of the stony variety. They look like Earth rocks, but they feel different. They are heavier than Earth rocks. Another difference is that stony meteorites are often attracted to a magnet.

Iron meteorites are quite different from stony meteorites. They are three times heavier than most Earth rocks, and they look like metal. They are easily attracted to a magnet.

It is easier to find iron meteorites than stony

Iron meteorites that have been on Earth for a long time have a rusty appearance.

meteorites. Pure iron is very rare on Earth. So if someone finds a chunk of iron in a farm field, it is probably a meteorite.

Stony-iron meteorites are among the rarest types. They make up less than 1 percent of all known meteorites. One kind of stony-iron is very

A polished section of a stony-iron meteorite (left) shows half metal and half stony minerals. Sometimes stony-iron meteorites (right) can be cut so thin that light can pass through the crystals.

beautiful. It can be cut and polished to bring out lovely green crystals set in shiny metal. These meteorites are highly prized.

WHERE DO METEORITES COME FROM?

Most meteorites come from the asteroid belt, which lies between the orbits of Mars and Jupiter. Asteroids are small planet-

The asteroid Ida as photographed by the *Galileo* spacecraft.

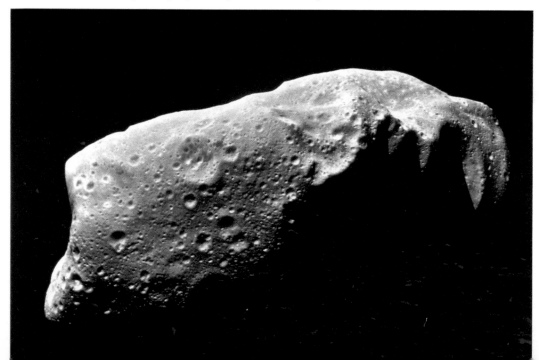

like bodies that orbit the sun. Sometimes they collide, and bits and pieces fly off in all directions. These small pieces continue to orbit the sun until they run into a planet like Earth.

A few unusual meteorites do not come from the asteroid belt. One kind comes from our moon. Another kind is believed to come from Mars.

Both the moon and Mars have been hit by objects

The moon (left) has been hit by countless objects throughout its history. The meteorite at right was blasted off the moon's surface by a giant impact and fell to Earth.

of all sizes. When an asteroid or a large meteoroid strikes them, it makes a crater. The impact can also blast rocks off the surface and into space. In time, these rocks could fall to Earth.

IMPACT CRATERS

Earth has been hit by meteorites countless times. Only the largest ones make craters, however. Hundreds of such meteorite craters can be seen all over the world.

The most famous crater is Meteor Crater in Arizona. It was created over 20,000 years ago when an iron meteorite struck the Earth. The impact caused a great

Meteor Crater, Arizona. The crater is one of the best examples of meteorite impacts on Earth.

explosion that destroyed most of the meteorite. It also made a huge hole in the ground.

A kind of rock called tektite is formed during very large meteorite impacts. The blast that forms the crater often melts some of the surrounding rock. Drops of this liquid rock are hurled great distances. As they travel, they cool and turn to hard, glassy objects. When they fall back to Earth, they take on the form of meteorites.

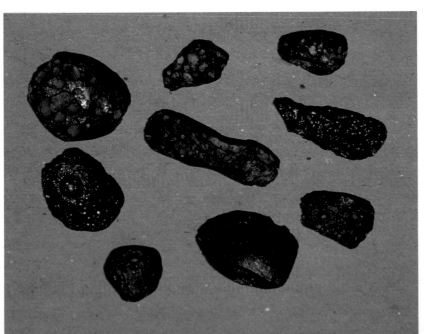

Tektites come in many different shapes and sizes.

LIFE FORMS AND METEORITES

Some scientists think that meteorite impacts may have changed life on Earth. When a very large meteorite hits Earth, it throws a large amount of dust into the atmosphere. This dust could block out sunlight for many months.

Most plants would die without sunlight. And many animals depend on plants for their food. Without

Corn (left) and other plants are a major source of food for animals. Many animals would die without plants for food. Big animals must eat large amounts of plants to survive.

plants to eat, the animals would die. Only life forms that can live without sunlight would survive. Plants and animals that die out are said to have become extinct.

Many scientists think that dinosaurs may have become extinct because of a meteorite impact. Scientists know that a giant impact occurred at about the time the dinosaurs disappeared. Could another giant impact change life on Earth again? No one knows for sure.

Opposite page: Many scientists believe that some dinosaurs became extinct because they could not find enough plants to eat.

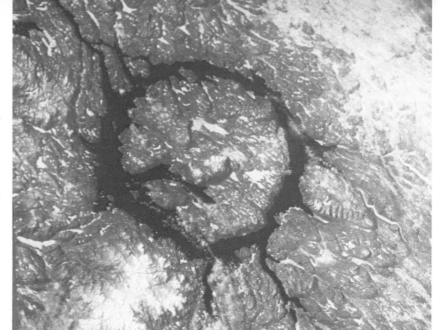

Manicouagan Crater in Canada, shown here as viewed from space, is one of the largest impact craters on Earth.

SCIENCE AND METEORITES

Why are scientists so interested in meteorites? Partly because meteorites are so much older than Earth rocks. In addition, meteorites are made up of many unusual minerals.

Some even contain diamonds. The chemistry of meteorites offers clues to the origin of Earth—and even to the beginning of life itself.

Meteorites were formed in a distant region of the solar system. Conditions there were very different from those on Earth. These differences caused some elements to form minerals that are unlike the minerals found in Earth rocks. Iron is one of those elements.

Hematite (top left) is a common iron mineral on Earth. A form of magnetite called lodestone (bottom left) is a natural magnet. A cut and polished slice of an iron meteorite (above) shows its different minerals.

On Earth, iron usually joins with oxygen to form minerals like hematite and magnetite.

Iron in meteorites combines with nickel to form the minerals kamacite and taenite. These are rare minerals on Earth.

Another interesting difference between a meteorite and an Earth rock is the presence of nickel. Almost every meteorite contains some nickel. But most Earth rocks only have very small amounts of nickel.

The stony type of meteorite is very important to science. One kind contains little round beadlike objects called

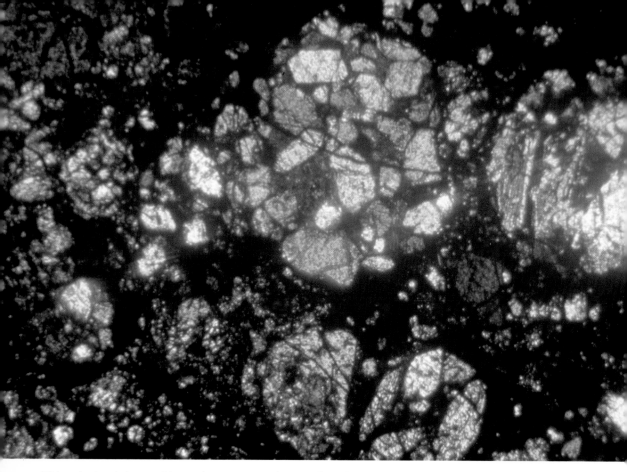

This photo, taken with a microscope, shows chondrules in a stony meteorite.

chondrules. These
chondrules are believed to
be the first solid objects
formed in the solar
system. That was over 4.6
billion years ago!

Another fascinating stony meteorite is called a carbonaceous chondrite. It is often as black as coal due to its carbon content.

Carbon is an important element for life—all living things contain carbon. Carbonaceous chondrite meteorites contain some of the same chemical compounds we have in our bodies. Some scientists believe that meteorites may have brought chemicals to Earth that enabled life on our planet to begin.

The Allende meteorite is an example of a carbonaceous chondrite.

HOW ARE METEORITES FOUND?

A scientist searches for iron meteorites with a metal detector.

Meteorites are not easy to find. Once they have been on Earth for a while, they look like ordinary rocks. So your chances of finding a meteorite are better in places where there are no other rocks, such as deserts or farm fields.

Very few people ever see a meteorite land. But if you are among the lucky ones, you can just pick it up.

37

When farmers remove rocks from their fields, they sometimes find meteorites.

Most meteorites are found by accident long after they fall. Farmers plowing their fields often find strange rocks. They may take these rocks to a museum or a university, where they can be properly identified.

In 1492, scientists first tried to explain the strange

stones that fell from the sky. Since then, about 3,000 meteorites have been found around the world. But that number does not include Antarctica's meteorites.

This huge meteorite was discovered in China in the 1980s. Scientists think it fell to Earth about 1400 years ago.

METEORITES IN ANTARCTICA

Thousands of meteorites have been found in Antarctica. By studying them, scientists learn more about the role meteorites played in the formation of our Solar System.

Why are so many meteorites found in Antarctica? The climate is one major reason. In areas where temperatures change from hot to cold, meteorites erode quickly. But cold temperatures slow down

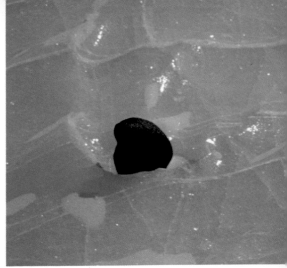

Scientists (left) find a small stony meteorite in Antarctica.
This small stony meteorite (right) was preserved by the cold
of Antarctica.

a meteorite's erosion
rate–and it is always very
cold in Antarctica. So
Antarctica is a natural
"storehouse" for meteorites.

Running water also speeds
up erosion. But it does
not play an important part
in Antarctica, where most
of the water is frozen.

LEARNING MORE

Would you like to learn more about meteorites? Most science museums and planetariums have meteorites on display. And

your local library has many

Searching among rocks may turn up a meteorite. Careful inspection (right) is needed to identify meteorites.

books on astronomy and geology to help you.

Perhaps you can try to find a meteorite on your own. All you need is a magnet, a good pair of eyes, and a curious mind.

Spring is the best time of year to look for meteorites. A great place to begin your meteorite hunt is along the sides of farm fields, where farmers pile up the rocks they find. But don't forget to ask for permission before you begin.

If you are not lucky enough to find a meteorite—and few people are—you can always buy one. A small iron meteorite is not very expensive.

Under a microscope, the secrets of how meteorites formed can be discovered.

A meteorite is a wondrous thing. When you hold it in your hand, think about where it came from. Think about how old it is. Some of the chemicals in your body may have come from a meteorite. We are all part of the universe.

WORDS YOU SHOULD KNOW

Antarctica (ant • ARK • tih • ka)–a large landmass around the South
Pole, covered by ice sheets

asteroids (AST • er • oydz)–small, planetlike objects that orbit the
sun between Mars and Jupiter

astronomy (ast • RAH • nuh • mee)–the study of the planets, stars,
and other heavenly bodies

atmosphere (AT • muss • feer)–the gases surrounding the earth
and some other planets; the air

carbon (KAR • bun)–a chemical element found in all plants and animal

carbonaceous (kar • buh • NAY • shus)–containing carbon

chemicals (KEM • ih • kilz)–elements that combine to make substance
found in nature

chemistry (KEM • iss • tree)–the science that studies what substances
are made of, how they combine with other substances,
and how they behave under certain conditions

chondrite (KAHN • drite)–a meteoritic stone that contains chondrules

chondrules (KAHN • droolz)–round, beadlike objects that are found
in some stony meteorites ·

comet (KAH • mit)–an object made of ice, gas, and dust that has a
long, glowing tail when near the sun

compound (KAHM • pownd)–a chemical substance formed by two
or more elements

constellation (kahn • stel • LAY • shun)–a group of stars that form a
pattern in a certain area of the sky

crater (KRAY • ter)–a bowl-shaped hole in the ground formed by a
volcano or a meteorite impact

crystal (KRISS • til)–a geometric shape that can form when a liquid
substance hardens

dinosaur (DY • nuh • sawr)–a group of extinct animals that dominated
the Earth many millions of years ago

erosion (ih • ROH • zjun)–a wearing away caused by the action of
wind and water

exposure (ex • POH • zjer)–the state of being unprotected, as from the weather

frictional heat (FRIK • shun • il HEET)–energy created by contact between two objects

fusion (FYOO • zjun)–a process of melting, caused by the application of heat

geology (jee • AH • luh • jee)–the study of Earth's features and history

hematite (HEM • ah • tite)–a mineral that contains iron and oxygen

kamacite (KAM • uh • site)–a mineral consisting of a blend of nickel and iron

magnet (MAG • nit)–a substance that has the power to draw iron or steel to it

magnetite (MAG • nih • tite)–a mineral that contains iron and oxygen and is attracted to a magnet

meteor (MEE • tee • or)–a piece of rock or metal that travels through Earth's atmosphere

meteorite (MEE • tee • or • ite)–a meteor that has hit Earth

meteoroid (MEE • tee • or • oid)–a small piece of rock or metal that travels through the Solar System

mineral (MIN • er • il)–a solid, crystalline material usually made up of two or more elements

nickel (NIK • il)–a shiny, silvery-white metal

orbit (OR • biht)–the path an object takes when it moves around another object

oxygen (AHX • ih • jin)–a gas found in the air

Perseid (PER • see • id)–having to do with Perseus, a constellation in the night sky

planet (PLAN • it)–a large cold object that orbits a star; the sun has nine planets

Solar System (SO • ler SISS • tim)–the sun and its "family" of planets, asteroids, and comets

star (STAHR)–a giant ball of hot, glowing gases

taenite (TAY • nite)–a mineral that is a blend of nickel and iron

tektite (TEHK • tite)–a glassy stone formed from melted rock after a meteorite impact

universe (YOO • nih • vers)–all of space and everything in it

INDEX

About the Author

Paul P. Sipiera is a professor of geology and astronomy at William Rainey Harper College in Palatine, Illinois. His principal areas of research are in the study of meteorites and volcanic rocks from New Zealand. He participated in the United States Antarctic Research Program during the 1983-84 field season as part of the Antarctic Search for Meteorites Program. His many professional activities include membership in the Explorers Club, the New Zealand Antarctic Society, and serving as president of the Planetary Studies Foundation. When he is not studying science, he can be found traveling the world or working on his farm in Galena, Illinois, with his wife Diane and their two daughters Andrea and Paula Frances.